THAT'S A JOB?

I Like the PERFORMING ARTS

... what jobs are there?

by Steve Martin

Illustrated by Roberto Blefari

Kane Miller
A DIVISION OF EDC PUBLISHING

CONTENTS

Music agent 28

Media and entertainment lawyer 29

Screenwriter 30

Critic 31

Location scout 32

Pop singer 34

Music producer 35

Choreographer 36

Ballet dancer 37

Vlogger 38

Movie director 40

Radio DJ 42

Session musician 43

Your perfect job match 44

There's more ... 46

INTRODUCTION

Qualities and skills for working in the performing arts

There are lots of jobs that involve working in the performing arts, some of which you may not even know existed.

Do you dream of starring on the big screen, or striding across a stage as an audience claps and cheers you on? Are creativity, entertainment, and teamwork important to you? If so, a career in the performing arts could be just right for you.

From working in music and dance, to technology and teaching, there are many jobs out there for those who want to shine in the spotlight or work behind the scenes.

Each job needs different people with different skills: screenwriters need strong imaginations and good writing skills; lawyers must have specialist knowledge; camera operators need to be technically minded; movie directors, artistic directors, and music producers need confidence to lead and inspire others.

But there are some qualities that everyone who works in the performing arts should have: a motivated, energized attitude, and a desire to create something special that others will enjoy and remember.

Being able to take criticism and listen to others are important skills, too. For instance, actors have to pick themselves up after unsuccessful auditions, and costume designers, visual effects artists, and set designers all have to follow briefs and take in feedback. Sometimes you might need patience—vloggers have to build their followers, ballet dancers spend endless hours practicing, and good stand-up comics spend months perfecting their routines.

Whatever the job, it's important to remember that it's not all about fame, fortune, or the finished product: it's about making connections, developing skills, and having fun!

If this sounds like you, then you're the right type of person to work in the performing arts!

This book looks at 25 different jobs that involve working in the performing arts, giving you a sneak peek into a typical day in the life of each worker. You'll learn the important stuff, like what it takes to get the job, and what duties and tasks are involved, and you'll discover the fun stuff too, such as the worst part of a makeup artist's job ...

HINT: It involves people who can't sit still!

When you've read about all the different jobs in the book, turn to page 44 to find out which jobs might suit you, or page 46 to discover even more jobs!

PROFESSIONAL ACTOR

Our job is to tell stories by portraying and bringing different characters to life. It's an exciting and varied career, and each of us loves what we do. But it takes a lot of hard work, talent, and commitment to be successful.

THEATER ACTOR

For me, nothing beats acting in front of a live audience. In high school, I loved drama class, and after starring in my first school play, I caught the acting bug! I majored in drama in college, and after graduating, I spent a few years acting on stage in supporting roles. After impressing directors and critics, I started to get lead parts, and today I star in all kinds of plays and musicals. Stamina and a good memory are key, since I have to remember my lines and perform for hours most days of the week, but nothing beats the rush of the stage and the spotlight!

TELEVISION ACTOR

Growing up, I was always good at doing impressions and making my friends laugh. After high school, I took an improvisation class—and I loved it! I took acting classes to develop my skills, and got experience with my local community theater. I signed up to casting websites, got an agent (who helped me find more auditions), and some experience as an extra (background actor). This helped me meet television producers, and eventually, I landed a recurring part in a comedy TV series. Over time, this led to more parts in other TV shows. I love working in television because unlike a movie, I often don't know how my character's story will unfold, and I also get to spend longer portraying a character, since a series might run for many seasons.

MOVIE ACTOR

I spend my days reading scripts, preparing
for roles, traveling to locations, and acting in movies.
I also promote the movies I work on through interviews
with the media. It's my dream job, but it took time to get here.
I earned a degree in acting, attended many auditions, learned skills to
make me stand out, like dance and horseback riding, and took any parts
I could get at first, no matter how small. It can be a demanding job, since
I often have to work long hours, face criticism, and sometimes have to
change my appearance for a role. But I love the challenge!

COSTUMED PERFORMER

My job lets me combine my two favorite
things—acting and working with children. I work
at a large theme park, where I dress as a popular
cartoon character and walk the park, interacting
with the visitors. I'm a "face" character, which
means I talk to visitors, too—but I have to
be in character at all times. I have scripts
and songs to learn, and must know my
character's whole backstory so that
I can be as convincing as possible.
Acting in school plays in high
school and taking singing lessons
helped me develop the skills
I needed for my job. It can be
stressful and tiring, since
I have to be able to think on
my feet and always need to be
full of energy and enthusiasm.
But nothing beats seeing how
excited the children get
when they see me!

VOICE ACTOR

When people ask me what movies or shows
they might see me in, they're often surprised when I say,
"None!" You don't "see" a voice actor onscreen; you hear
them. But this doesn't make my job any easier. Most actors
can use facial expressions and body language to help them act,
but I only get one tool—my voice! It took time and
effort to get my job: I had to take acting classes,
practice different voices and accents, and go to many
auditions before I started getting hired and building
my reputation. I love the variety of my job. One day
I'm playing Splurff, a cartoon Martian in a video
game, the next I'm doing the voiceover for a
soap commercial, or narrating an audiobook.

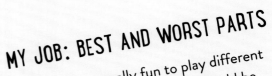

MY JOB: BEST AND WORST PARTS

BEST: It can be really fun to play different
roles—you get to see what life would be
like if you were a different person!

WORST: We often have to cope with a lot
of setbacks, like unsuccessful auditions,
long periods without work, or bad reviews.

DRAMA TEACHER

I've always wanted to work with children and young people, so after my theater studies degree, I earned my teaching certificate and started working at a local high school. I spend my days teaching acting skills, helping students develop confidence, and sharing my love of drama.

1

I start the day with my eleventh-grade students, working on their acting skills. I've split them into groups where they will act out a scene about a teenager returning home late, after curfew, to face their disappointed parents! Using relatable situations can help students to sympathize with their characters and act more naturally. Each group takes a turn to act the scene in front of the class, and I give them notes on their performance.

There are so many opportunities for those who love both teaching and the performing arts. There are music teachers, dance teachers, singing coaches, dialect coaches (people who help actors perform different accents), and more.

2

In my next lesson, I have the students try a few improvisation games. These games help them to loosen up, shake off shyness or embarrassment, and practice acting skills. In one of the games, I ask the students to perform a scene, but pretend to walk through a huge blob of floating jelly as they act. They have to use their body to show how the jelly might slow them down or stick to them!

3

In my next lesson, I play a video showing professional actors in a scene from William Shakespeare's *Macbeth*. As a class, we then discuss the language and time period of the play. It's not all acting; a big part of my job is to teach students about theater history and great drama from the past.

4

At lunchtime I hold auditions for our next school play, a production of the musical *Grease*. Managing and directing school plays takes up a lot of time and energy, but it's one of my favorite parts of the job. Plays are a chance for the school to come together, and lots of students take part as musicians, actors, or crew members. I make notes while I encourage the hopeful students who audition. I'll try to find a role for everyone.

5

An hour later, I'm with a ninth-grade class. I've prepared a lesson all about what goes into a stage production, from set design, to props, costumes, music, and lighting, as well as all the people needed behind the scenes. At the end of class, I give out a homework assignment based on today's lesson, and I warn the students that there will be a quiz on it next week. That causes a few students to grumble!

7

The school day is over, but I don't head home just yet. Tonight, I have parent-teacher conferences, where I talk about my students and their progress in class. It's a chance to update their adults and put plans in place for any students who may need extra help or support.

6

The rest of my afternoon is free, so I use the time to grade homework, review my notes from today's auditions, and write lesson plans for next week. Being organized and preparing in advance is important in my job.

8

I finally get home at 7:00 p.m. I turn on the TV and relax. It's nice to watch other people doing all the work for a change!

MY JOB: BEST AND WORST PARTS

BEST: I love running rehearsals—it's great to see students develop from the first rehearsal to opening night.

WORST: Sometimes I need to tell students they can't play their preferred part in a play or production. It's hard to see them disappointed.

MAKEUP ARTIST

My passion for makeup started during high school when I worked part-time at a makeup counter. I then went to cosmetology school where I developed my skills and learned about different products, skin care, sanitation, and more. Today, I'm a licensed cosmetologist (makeup artist) and I work on movie sets, transforming the actors, and bringing the directors' visions to life!

I worked my way up to my current position by volunteering with local drama groups and working on smaller jobs while I built connections and gained experience. Other makeup artists specialize in fashion, helping models—or anyone having photos taken for a special occasion—to look their best for photoshoots.

1

I'm working on a movie called *The Greatest Day*. It's the first day of filming, but I've been preparing for some time. As the key makeup artist on this job, I've already designed all the makeup looks and ordered the supplies. Today I'll be working on the lead actors, and supervising the other makeup artists and assistants as they work on the rest of the cast.

The Greatest Day

2

I arrive on set at 6:00 a.m. I'm always one of the first here because the actors need to be "made up" before filming starts. I have a schedule to work to and it's best to be organized, so my day starts with preparing my equipment in the makeup trailer and making sure the rest of my team is ready to start, too.

3

At 7:00 a.m., Monica, one of the movie's lead actors, arrives. We chat while I apply her makeup. It's important to get along with people in my job. I check photos and notes I've made of my designs as I work, to make sure the final look is as planned. The movie is set in the 1940s, so I spent a lot of time researching what people looked like then when I created my designs.

4

Next up is the other lead actor, Juan. He has a tattoo on his neck that I need to cover up for his character, and I also need to apply subtle, natural makeup to his face. All the actors need makeup—otherwise the studio lights and high-quality cameras would highlight every little bruise or blemish.

5

I check in with my team and make sure they're on track. We have to work quickly, since the cast also need to visit the hair and wardrobe departments before filming.

6

I continue applying makeup throughout the day. Sometimes I stand by on set, to touch up the actors' makeup, and other times I work in the trailer. During quiet moments I order more supplies.

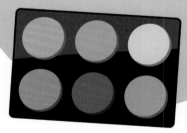

7

Later, Monica returns for her second look of the day. In her next scene, we see her character in the future, so she needs to look much, much older. This is a job for our special-effects makeup artist—he is on hand for more complex looks like this where the actors need to look older, injured, or even nonhuman! I watch as he uses prosthetics to transform Monica's face. The result is amazing!

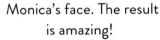

8

As the filming comes to an end, the actors stop by the trailer so we can remove the makeup and prosthetics. All that's left to do is tidy up and head home. I'll be back tomorrow for another jam-packed day.

MY JOB: BEST AND WORST PARTS

BEST: I love watching actors transform as I use my artistic skills to change the way they look.

WORST: I know it can be hard to sit still, but it's challenging when people don't!

SET DESIGNER

I spend my days designing sets for theater productions. It's a little different than working on TV or movie sets because I have less space and less time to work with, but I love the challenge! A good set helps to create atmosphere and tell the story. I need a real mix of creative, technical, and practical skills in my job, since I have to imagine exciting new designs, but I also have to consider factors like materials, health and safety, and space.

To get my job, I earned a degree in theater design, then spent time working in smaller theaters, and assisting other designers. Now that I have a good reputation, I'm hired to design sets for bigger productions.

1

For the last month I've been designing the sets for a 1950s rock 'n' roll musical. At the start of the project, I read the script and worked with the director to understand his vision and decide how many sets were needed. I've already researched, designed, and made models of two sets (a diner and a dance hall), and this morning I'm showing the director my sketches for the third set—a street scene.

2

I show the director my work. I've spent more time researching the 1950s to make sure the buildings, signs, and street look accurate for the era. The director loves my ideas! Over the next few days, I'll build a model of this set, too, to show exactly how the stage will look and where the scenery and props will be. Once all the models are approved, we'll start building the sets.

3

Next, I talk with the carpenter. She's building some furniture for the diner set. I explain that the tables need to be strong and sturdy, since the performers will be dancing on top of them! I also ask her to build the seats in a particular shape, so that we can reuse them along the walls of the dance hall set. I have a budget for the sets, and reusing items like this is a good way to keep costs down.

4

I drive across town to the dance studio to talk with the choreographer for the dance routines. It's important that I leave enough room on each set for the dancers to move safely. I discuss the street set with him, and he gives me a video of the dancers rehearsing. I'll use this to help me refine the model.

5

Back at the theater, I check on the set painter. The director wants the play to be light, fun, and full of energy, so we need vibrant colors in the diner. She's using lots of bright yellow and red, so I'm happy. The dance hall will be plainer, but the cast's costumes will bring it to life.

6

In the afternoon I meet with the lighting designer. Some of the street scenes will be at night, and I'd like streetlights to be part of the set design. He advises that two lights, one on each side of the stage, should be enough. I'm starting to get really excited about how the play is going to look!

7

My last task is to meet with the prop master. Props are items that aren't scenery or costumes, and the prop master is in charge of making, buying, or renting them. We need lots of props for this production, including a jukebox and fake ice cream sundaes. We look at old photographs from the 1950s to choose the right designs.

8

At home, I spend the evening rereading the script. I'm a little worried because the break between the diner scene and the street scene is very short. I'll speak to the carpenter in the morning to see if she can fit hidden wheels on the furniture to make it easier to move. Problem-solving is a big part of my job!

MY JOB: BEST AND WORST PARTS

BEST: Every play, opera, and musical is different—one day I'm designing a spooky haunted house with trapdoors, the next, I'm figuring out how to get a swimming pool on stage!

WORST: I work for myself, and the pressure to constantly find more work can be tough.

STAND-UP COMIC

Growing up, I loved to make my friends laugh. After high school, I took comedy classes and started writing and performing routines at comedy clubs. It took me a few years to find my style, but gradually I built up my reputation and my success grew and grew. Now I'm a well-known stand-up comic, and I get paid to perform my routines in front of live audiences all over the country.

As a successful, full-time stand-up comic, I spend a lot of time on tour performing long routines. But I also visit smaller clubs to practice new material. Not all comedians enjoy facing a live audience. Some prefer to work as comedy writers—writing jokes for other people, or writing comedy sketches and shows for TV.

1

Tonight I'm performing at a comedy club in Los Angeles. It's the first show in a 30-stop tour across California and Nevada. A stand-up comic has to do a lot of traveling! I arrive at my hotel in the afternoon and spend time going over my routine. There's nothing worse than forgetting your lines when you're standing in front of hundreds of people.

2

My act is a mix of jokes, funny stories, and observations. Often the stories are made up or exaggerated to be as funny as possible. I rehearse in front of the mirror. Stand-up comics need to be good actors because the jokes have to sound natural, and the timing needs to be right. Sometimes, a pause at the right moment can guarantee a laugh.

3

On my way to the club, I overhear a little boy ask his mom why you can get popcorn but not mom-corn. I whip out my notebook and write that down to make into a joke later. As a comic, I always write down funny things I hear or see—coming up with new jokes is the hardest part of the job!

4

I get changed at the club. My stage character is a lovable guy who tries to be cool but gets everything wrong. He's a little bit like the real me, if I'm honest! Some stand-up comics don't have characters and just perform as themselves, while others have multiple characters.

5

I'm the headline act, which means I'll go on last after the other stand-up comics. From the side of the stage, I watch another comic perform before me. She does impressions of famous people, and she's really funny, which will help to put the audience in the right mood for my act. Getting to watch other comics for free is a real perk of the job.

6

It's showtime! I take to the stage and soon have the audience laughing. Confidence is key—if the audience senses your nerves, it's harder to win them over. My performance goes really well. It's my first time performing this particular routine, so I'm thrilled with the reaction. There was only one heckler, who yelled out in the middle of my routine, but I had my responses ready. The best way to deal with a heckler is to be funnier than they are!

7

After the performance, I stay back to talk to members of the audience. It's important to be respectful and show your audience you care, so I always make sure to take pictures and thank people for coming.

8

Back at the hotel, I go over my routine again. There were one or two jokes that didn't get the laughs I expected. I don't take it personally; I learn from it. In this job you have to have a thick skin. I'll keep tinkering with the act during the tour to make sure it's the best it can be.

MY JOB: BEST AND WORST PARTS

BEST: Nothing beats hearing the audience burst into laughter at one of my jokes.

WORST: The silence when a joke doesn't land feels like it lasts forever.

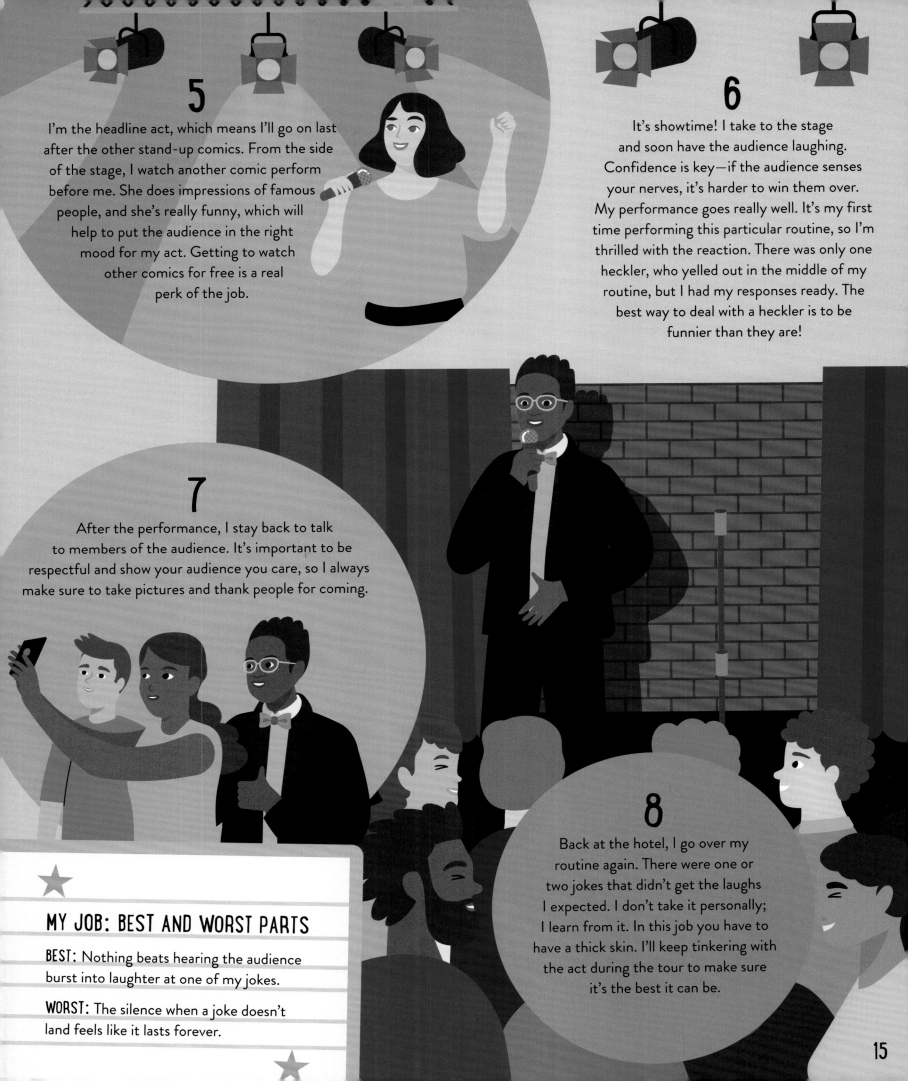

CAMERA OPERATOR

I set up and operate the cameras used to film TV shows, commercials, and movies. After earning a degree in film production, I started as a production assistant, running errands and doing anything else that was asked. This gave me experience working in TV studios and on location. Today, I'm employed by a TV production company to work on a children's drama series.

Camera operators work closely with cinematographers, who help the director decide how each shot will look. Some camera operators become "specialist operators," and train to film in specific, often daring situations. There are underwater camera operators, and operators who film while jumping out of planes!

1

I arrive on site where we are shooting an evening scene for *Sunnyvale Junior High*. We're filming on location, which means we're on a real-life street that we have all to ourselves. Camera operators work when and where they're needed, so I'm used to traveling and working late.

2

After unloading my equipment, I speak with the director. She's in charge of the production and explains how she wants the scene to look. I pay close attention—listening skills are so important in my role.

3

The scene is an exciting chase. Sometimes we use cranes to film from above or tracks to smoothly move the camera and follow the action. But today, the director wants me to film from the side of the street, showing the actors running by. I consider the best spot, then position the camera on a stand called a tripod. Other days, I have to run after the actors while filming them!

MY JOB: BEST AND WORST PARTS

BEST: It's great being part of a team, and I love working with new and ever-changing technology.

WORST: Working with heavy equipment is physically tough—I have to work hard to keep fit and strong.

4

The director wants the background to look blurred, so I choose a lens and adjust the camera settings to achieve this. Different lenses and settings allow for different angles and effects in the shot—they can make things look blurry or in focus, close-up or wide and open. My experience means I know how to get the exact effect the director is looking for.

5

Next, I run a camera test to see if the equipment, settings, and location I've chosen are right for this scene. The test shows that the lighting is too dark to see the action. I let the director know, and we speak to the lighting technician. We're all part of a team, and we each have our own expertise. With a few adjustments of the camera and lighting, we're ready to shoot.

6

I film from the side, while another camera operator films from the end of the street, with the actors running toward him. I watch the action carefully, making sure I keep the actors in the frame as I turn the camera to follow them. This is called "panning." There are lots of techniques like this to make scenes look as exciting as possible.

7

After we've filmed from this angle, the director decides to try filming on a track, after all. I help set up the track, run more tests, then we start shooting. Knowing the equipment inside and out means I can adapt to unexpected changes.

8

Later, the film editor will cut and merge my shots with the other camera operator's using special computer software, so the viewer sees one fluid chase scene from several angles. It's rewarding to see how our skills behind the cameras bring a scene to life onscreen.

17

STUNT ARTIST

My days are action-packed: you can find me dangling from helicopters, rappelling down buildings, and much more. It's my job to fill in for actors and perform risky stunts. It's not easy—I have to be very fit and brave, and I need to have lots of skills, such as horseback riding, gymnastics, and martial arts. I'm good at parkour (jumping and climbing over obstacles), so I get a lot of work chasing people and being chased!

I went to a stunt school to train and learn how to perform stunts safely, then worked as an apprentice to a professional stunt artist, learning from his example for a few years. Today, I'm hired to perform all kinds of stunts for movies, TV shows, and commercials.

1

This morning, I'm on the set of an action movie. The hairstylist is fitting me with a wig so I can look more like the lead actress, who has brown hair. The final, edited film won't show my face, but I still need to look as much like the actress as possible.

2

Next, I visit the wardrobe department to get dressed. I'm usually on set all day, but only a small part of that time involves filming the actual stunts. I need to be patient in my job. There's so much preparation.

3

I meet up with the stunt coordinator. I've worked with him on lots of films, and we're good friends. He talks me through how he wants the stunt to work. I'm going to be driving a speedboat and leaping from it onto the sand.

4

We spend the next two hours rehearsing. We're also going to blow up the speedboat, and we've only got one, so there will be no second takes! Everything must be perfect the first time around.

5

Finally, we're ready to go. The rescue boat and firefighters are on standby. Safety always comes first in stunt work.

6

There is a camera on the beach, one on a boat, and another filming from a helicopter. I open the throttle and the speedboat roars across the sea, bouncing over the waves. I turn in a half circle and accelerate straight up onto the beach.

7

As I leap from the boat, the special effects technicians set off the explosion. I dive forward as if thrown off my feet by the blast. A stunt artist is also an actor— anyone can fall down, but only a stunt artist can make it look good, and do it safely!

8

The crew gather together afterward, and we watch the recordings. I grin from ear to ear when everyone gives me a round of applause. That's another job well done, and it's time to go home. What a day!

MY JOB: BEST AND WORST PARTS

BEST: I love all the thrills in my job.

WORST: Even the most careful stunt artist can get hurt. And it's not a career you can do forever.

SOUND ENGINEER

I loved working for my high school radio station, so I studied music production in college. I learned all about sound engineering, electronics, acoustics, recording, and editing. After graduation, I started working as a live sound engineer, handling the sound at events, such as concerts and theater performances. For the past month, I've been on tour with The Screaming Eagles, one of my favorite rock bands. It's my job to travel with them and help them sound great at every show!

I love the excitement of my job—I work in live situations, so I have to think on my feet and solve problems quickly. Many sound engineers prefer to work in recording studios, while others work in TV and radio.

1

Tonight the band is playing at a concert hall in Texas. There's a huge amount of equipment to unload from the truck. Luckily, the road crew do all the heavy lifting while I supervise! Once it's inside, it's up to me to set up the cables, speakers, mixing equipment, and microphones.

2

Once everything is ready, I carry out a sound check. This is where the band plays a couple of songs so I can check that the vocals and instruments can be heard perfectly. It's also a chance to see if any equipment is faulty. There's noisy feedback from one of the speakers, so I quickly fix the problem.

MY JOB: BEST AND WORST PARTS

BEST: My technical skills can turn a good show into something spectacular.

WORST: Traveling means a lot of time away from my family, and the late nights can be tiring.

3

Soon it's time for the concert to start. While the band brings the house down with their music, I monitor the quality of the sound, making changes to keep it as good as it can be. The fans have a great evening.

4

The concert is over, but my job's not! As I pack all the gear, I think about tomorrow's concert. It's going to be outside in a park, so I need to consider all the challenges and logistics of that type of venue. I'm used to it, though!

LIGHTING TECHNICIAN

I work in-house at a large theater where people come to watch plays, musicals, and other performances. It's my job to set up, operate, check, and repair the lighting equipment. I earned a degree in electrical engineering and started out as a lighting assistant before I got my current job. I love using my skills to help produce amazing spectacles.

1

Tonight is opening night for a new play, but my work starts much earlier in the day. The cast and crew have been preparing for weeks, including rehearsing the lighting plan, but I still spend time checking the lights again today.

2

During my checks, I notice that one of the lights isn't working! I lower it so I can investigate what's wrong. Luckily, it's just a bad bulb, so I replace it. Sometimes there can be problems with the wiring, which can take longer to fix.

Part of my job is to work with my teammates in the lighting department, including the lighting director, who creates lighting plans for each production. The plan includes what effects, colors, and types of lights will be used, as well as the positioning, sequence, and timings they will be used in.

3

Most of the lighting is already in position around the stage, but some lights will be brought on and off during scene changes, so I make sure to test those lights, too. Once I'm happy that everything is ready and working, I let the lighting director know, and then I take a break before the show begins.

4

Soon, the audience are in their seats, and it's time to shine! I'm sitting at the lighting desk, where I can operate the lights. Through my headset, the production manager gives me my cue, so I dim the lights, and everyone quiets down. The opening scene begins with a spotlight on center stage.

5

I concentrate hard throughout the performance, following the plan just like we rehearsed. The lighting has to change at key moments, so if I mistime it, it could ruin a scene. Luckily, it all runs smoothly, and the show is a great success! I help turn off and pack away the equipment before I head home. I'll be back in the morning to do it all again, but for now, it's lights-out!

MY JOB: BEST AND WORST PARTS

BEST: Lighting plays a huge role in creating the right atmosphere, and I love being a part of it.

WORST: I usually work evenings and weekends, so it can be hard to spend time with friends outside of work.

VISUAL EFFECTS ARTIST

Some things are impossible or impractical to film in real life, such as an explosion that destroys a building—it would be dangerous, costly, and messy—so that's where I come in! I use creative and computer skills to help build imaginary worlds and create amazing illusions, which look real. My work is then combined with live-action footage to make enthralling and believable movies.

There are different kinds of visual effects artists, but I specialize as an animator. This means I use software to create moving characters and objects with CGI (computer-generated imagery). Earning a degree in animation taught me lots of skills that helped me get my job, including how to use special computer software.

1

I arrive at the office and greet my colleagues. I work for a large visual effects studio, which is hired to help directors turn their visions into reality. I work on movies, but other animators work on TV shows and computer games. Today, I'm working on bringing a monster called Squidzilla to life for a new movie. Squidzilla is a giant, man-eating squid, and it's my job to make it look, move, and act convincing.

2

I start the day meeting with my supervisor, the concept artist who drew the first sketches of the monster (based on the movie director's brief), and the modeling artist who created a basic digital 3D model. Over the last couple of weeks, I've used their groundwork to develop Squidzilla's character, perfecting details, colors, textures, and other characteristics. I show them my progress, and I'm pleased to get approval to start working on the motions and expressions of the monster. Most projects need a team of visual effects artists to work together, so it's important to be a good team player.

3

At my workstation, I reread the storyboard (this tells me how the scene in the movie should look). The director wants the monster to rise to the ocean's surface, wrap its tentacles around the boat, and drag it under the water! It's my job to make the monster move in a realistic and believable way.

SPECIAL EFFECTS

Special effects are different than visual effects. They are practical effects that are used during live-action filming or performances. They include things like prosthetic makeup, mechanical models, and pyrotechnics.

4

I begin by researching how real squid move in the ocean, how their tentacles and suckers work, calculating the right speeds, and so on. I must get every detail perfect, including the tiniest muscle movement or blink. If it isn't exactly right, the monster will look fake in the movie. Researching like this is a big part of my job. In the past I've had to find out how tornados travel, how dinosaurs run, and more!

5

In the afternoon, I use my research and special computer software to begin making the 3D model move. Sometimes our team will use motion capture software, too. This is where real actors are filmed wearing suits that record their movements and expressions, which are then transferred to CGI characters.

6

The visual effects manager drops by to check on my work. She gives me a few notes and things to improve. Listening to feedback helps make sure the finished work is the best it can be. She also tells me that the movie director wants to review our progress next week. The pressure's on, since it's not a lot of time, but tight deadlines are just a part of the job!

7

My afternoon ends with a training session. The studio has bought a new CGI software package, and all the visual effects artists need to learn how to use it. This industry is really cutting-edge, so it's important to stay up-to-date like this.

8

Soon it's the end of the day. I'll be back tomorrow to continue working on Squidzilla, but this evening I'm meeting up with friends to watch a movie—it's one I worked on, and I can't wait to see how the audience reacts to the CGI aliens!

MY JOB: BEST AND WORST PARTS

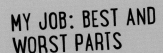

BEST: I love that my job helps moviemakers achieve the impossible!

WORST: I sometimes have to work very long hours to hit deadlines.

DANCE COMPANY ARTISTIC DIRECTOR

I started my career as a dancer, then worked as a choreographer for many years before getting my job as the artistic director of Fusion Dance, a contemporary dance company. Our mission is to bring dance to as many people in as many places as possible, and it's my job to lead the company and help make that happen.

Our dance company tours the country, putting on dance performances for audiences. We also hold performances for private parties and events, organize workshops and special performances for local schools, and offer dance classes for the public. Other dance companies tour internationally, too.

1

This morning, I'm in my office planning the program for next season. As the artistic director, I get to choose what themes to explore, and this year the main theme will be "The Natural World." I'm commissioning some brand-new dances, but I also need to select existing company dances that fit the theme. I look through our repertoire (collection of dances) and start making a list. Once the list is finished, I'll share it with the choreographers and dancers.

The Natural World

2

I take a break to think about the tour. The company will be traveling around the country performing the dances, and I need to find the right venues—theaters and spaces with big stages. We often revisit the same venues, but this year I want as many outdoor venues as possible to fit with the theme. There's a lot to plan and organize, but I love a challenge! Luckily, my years in the business have helped me make lots of contacts, and I start reaching out right away.

3

My last task of the morning is to interview a choreographer. It's part of my job to hire creative and technical staff, including dancers, choreographers, and dance directors, and I'm always looking for talented people to join our team. The interview goes well; the choreographer has excellent experience, and her work is full of passion and creativity. I offer her the job, and I'm thrilled when she accepts.

4

At lunch, I head out to meet with a composer (someone who writes music). I love his work, and I've hired him to write the music for one of the new dances. I explain that the dance will be about the seasons, and the composer suggests that each season highlight a different musical instrument. We share ideas, and he agrees to send me an update next week. Getting to use my creative skills and work with other artists is a great part of my job!

5

Next, I head to a local theater. Fusion Dance organizes special daytime performances for school students to attend, and there is one happening today. These performances help young people to discover and fall in love with dance. Afterward, the students ask me questions about dance, and our company, and we take a picture together. As the artistic director, it's part of my job to be the face of the company—attending events, meeting the community, and promoting the dance company.

6

Back in my office, I spend time doing paperwork, and calling and emailing potential sponsors. These are businesses and individuals who donate money to the dance company, which helps us fund our work.

7

Soon it's the end of the day. Tomorrow will be just as busy! I have a meeting with the costume designer to discuss the dances for next season and a meeting with the accountant to make sure we're on budget. Even though I'm not dancing anymore, I still need lots of energy in this job!

MY JOB: BEST AND WORST PARTS

BEST: I love using my leadership and organizational skills.

WORST: Making sure the company is making enough money to pay the dancers and staff can be stressful.

25

COSTUME DESIGNER

I've always loved fashion—when I watched movies as a kid, it was the costumes that caught my attention. As a teenager, I worked part-time in a costume store, and my favorite hobby was making my own clothes. After high school, I studied costume design in college. Now I spend my days designing costumes for movies—just like the ones I used to watch!

1

This morning I'm meeting the director and producer of a new movie I've been hired to work on, called *The Silent Highwayman*. I've already read the script, and made lots of notes, and I'm excited to find out more!

My job is to design, create, and hire costumes for different movies. My work helps tell the story of a movie, and it also helps the actors to get into character. I work closely with directors, assistant costume designers, hair and makeup teams, costume makers, and suppliers, like fabric and clothing stores. Other costume designers create costumes for theater productions or TV shows.

2

The director explains her vision for the movie. She wants a dark, scary atmosphere, and I'll need to reflect this in the color and style of the costumes. We also talk about the characters, the setting, and the time period—the movie is set in the 1700s, and the director is keen for the costumes to look realistic. Soon, I've got a good idea of what the director wants, and I can't wait to get started.

3

I head to the library and check out a few books on fashion in the 1700s. I need to start researching the time period and find out what clothes people wore, as well as what materials were used. Research can be a huge part of my job, and I often visit libraries, museums, and galleries, and meet with historians and experts to make sure I get things right. Sometimes though, for example in fantasy movies, historical accuracy is less important, and I can really let my imagination run wild!

4

Back at home, I start reading the books, and do a little online research, too—it's fascinating! I create a mood board as I go, adding pictures, materials, and color swatches.

5

After lunch, I use what I've learned so far to make a start on some rough sketches. I'll refine these over the next few weeks, as I do more research. I begin with sketches of the main character. In the story, he rides a black horse, and is kind of a spooky figure. I sketch a long black coat so that he can blend in, in the dark!

The Silent Highwayman Costume Plot

Character	Scene 1	Scene 2	Scene 3
	Black coat Hat Boots		

6

I spend the rest of the afternoon working on the "costume plot"—this details what each character is wearing in each scene of the movie. Most of the main characters will have multiple costumes. Today, I concentrate on the first scene in the script and write notes on what I think the characters could wear. I have to consider where they are, the time of day, the personality of the character, and much more.

7

Soon it's the end of the day. The next few weeks will all be very similar. Once I've finished the sketches and costume plot, I'll present it to the director. But my job doesn't end once the sketches and costume plot are approved: I'll then be in charge of finding the materials, hiring costume makers, and arranging costume fittings for the cast. But all that's in the future!

8

After a day of reading, drawing, and writing, I unwind in my favorite way—at my sewing machine!

MY JOB: BEST AND WORST PARTS

BEST: I love the variety in my job. Some days I'm designing historic costumes, next it'll be princess dresses, and other times I'll work on amazing sci-fi outfits.

WORST: It is upsetting when costumes I've worked hard on get torn or damaged.

MUSIC AGENT

After getting a degree in music management, I joined a music agency as an intern. I worked my way up, got my license, and today I work with lots of talented artists. It's my job to schedule concerts and tours and manage everything that that entails, including negotiating fees and contracts. I spend most days on the phone, so good communication skills are vital!

Another name for my job is booking agent. I work with musicians, but other agents work with actors, athletes, and dancers. For all of us, our main responsibility is to handle things behind the scenes, so that our clients can focus on their passions.

1

My first meeting today is with a band called The Musketeers that I'm hoping to represent. I explain how I can help them schedule and manage their concerts in return for a percentage of the money they make. We get on well, and they agree to work with me—success!

2

After the meeting, I check my email. One of the bands I represent is playing at a festival tomorrow, but there's a problem: the organizers want the band to stay in a hotel much farther away than originally agreed. I call the organizers and politely explain that this isn't acceptable. They offer to arrange and pay for travel expenses, so, with the band's permission, I accept the compromise. I often have to negotiate like this to get the best for my clients.

3

Next, one of my clients, Linda, arrives at the office. We're planning a summer tour to promote her new album. She wants to do a lot of concerts, and she wants a mix of large venues and smaller, cozier ones. Luckily, I know a lot of concert promoters and venue managers! My job is all about building relationships with people.

4

After Linda leaves, I start emailing my contacts. I let them know the dates and requirements, such as what equipment will be needed and what's on Linda's rider. (A rider is a list of requests that artists want the venues or organizers to provide, such as food and transportation.) Linda always requests ice cream to help soothe her throat after singing! Each venue will sign a contract and pay Linda a fee to perform—the venues make money from ticket and refreshment sales.

MY JOB: BEST AND WORST PARTS

BEST: I love music, but I can't sing or play an instrument—this job lets me work in the industry in a way that suits my talents.

WORST: Most of my days are spent in an office, which can get a little dull.

5

I spend the rest of the day reviewing contracts and checking in with clients. After all that talking, I head home and follow Linda's lead by treating myself to a bowl of ice cream!

MEDIA AND ENTERTAINMENT LAWYER

I'm a people person, so what I love most about my job is feeling like I make a difference for my clients. I help people and companies resolve legal issues that relate to the media, including TV, movies, music, and book publishing. My work involves a lot of reading and analyzing, but it also requires confidence—I have to stand up for my clients and protect them.

I work at a law firm. To get my job, I had to graduate from college, then law school, and pass the bar exam. I represent individuals such as authors, musicians, and producers, as well as companies like movie studios, ad agencies, and publishers.

1

This morning I'm at a movie studio. One of my clients, a high-profile actor, is starring in a new movie, and I'm negotiating the best contract possible for him with the studio's lawyers. I need to make sure my client gets fair compensation for his work, and that he is happy with the terms. The meeting goes well; the studio agrees to the fee my client wants.

2

Back at the office, I'm helping another client—a book publisher—to stop a company selling illegal copies of one of their best-selling books. This is called breach of copyright and is a serious crime. First, I send a "cease and desist" letter ordering them to stop, and then we'll also take the company to court. If we win our case, the company will have to pay a big fine to my client. I start preparing by gathering the evidence, and filing the correct paperwork. Attention to detail is everything!

3

In the afternoon, I get a call from a different client. She's a well-known singer, and she's very upset because an online newspaper has printed a false story about her. Printing lies is called libel, and I will write to the paper and demand that they print an apology. It's my job to protect my clients' reputations and privacy as much as their creative property. I listen to her and answer her questions; helping clients understand the laws and their rights is key.

4

I finish my day with some reading and research. The media and entertainment industry is always changing. To give my clients the best advice, I have to keep my knowledge up-to-date and think about how to apply laws to new technology. I love the challenge!

MY JOB: BEST AND WORST PARTS

BEST: I've worked hard to become an expert, and I love using my knowledge to help clients.

WORST: I don't like getting people into trouble, but I do have to protect my clients.

SCREENWRITER

I love writing, and while studying creative writing in college, I realized my dream was to write and develop scripts for movies. After lots of hard work, I did it! Today, I create the dialogue, characters, and storyline for movies. Sometimes I come up with the story on my own, other times I adapt books, or true stories, and then sometimes producers reach out to me with an idea they want me to develop.

1

This morning, I'm pitching my new script idea to a Hollywood producer. Producers oversee the production of a movie—they find scripts, source funding, hire directors, and are often involved right up to the movie's release.

2

I go through the outline (breakdown of the story) and share the script. It's based on a true story about a young boy with a disability who becomes a surfing sensation. I had to do a lot of research and editing to get it just right. The producer loves it! She pays me a fee to option (rent) my script for a year, while she sees if she can get funding for it. If she can, she'll buy it from me for a bigger fee, and it will be made into a movie. There's a lot of waiting in my job!

Lots of people want to be screenwriters, and it takes luck, determination, and talent to succeed. I started out as a movie producer's assistant (and writing in the evenings), so I could learn about the industry and build connections. I then pitched my scripts to many producers before I got my break. These days, I've built my reputation and sold enough scripts that I can write full-time.

3

After the pitch, I go home and work on another script. I make sure to write for at least three hours every day.

4

Later, I get a call from a producer I've worked with before. He wants to hire me to write a script based on a popular novel about a young girl who discovers that her pet dog has magical powers! I tell him I'll read the novel and then decide. I have to love the story if I'm going to be able to make other people enjoy it.

5

I finish my day meeting with some other writers—there's a playwright (who writes stories for the theater), as well as another screenwriter. We meet once a month to share ideas, get feedback, and support each other. They're all thrilled that my pitch was a success!

MY JOB: BEST AND WORST PARTS

- **BEST:** It's wonderful to see my words come to life on the screen.

- **WORST:** Writer's block is the worst! It can be so stressful staring at a blank page when a deadline is looming.

CRITIC

Growing up I loved nothing more than going to the movies. I liked the experience of getting lost in the story and then talking about all the details with my friends. In high school, I wrote reviews for our school newspaper and went on to earn a college degree in cinema studies. These days, I'm a movie critic—I watch and review movies, and help audiences decide whether to go see them for themselves.

Not all critics review movies. Plays, TV shows, art shows, books, and even restaurants are regularly reviewed by different kinds of critics.

1

I'm a freelancer, which means I work for myself and sell my reviews to magazines, newspapers, and websites. Today my first task is reviewing a comedy movie for an entertainment website. The movie features a new actress, and she's hilarious, but the rest of the cast don't really shine. As I write, I make my tone witty and informal, since that's the style the website wants. Good writing skills are essential in my job.

2

Next up, I record a video reviewing an old scary movie from the '70s. I run a review channel on a video-sharing platform, and the more people that watch, the more I get paid for my work! So it's important that I keep the channel up-to-date with new material. Today I've invited another critic to discuss the movie with me, and it's fun to swap opinions and debate the movie.

3

My last job of the day is pretty great: I'm off to the premiere of a new superhero film. A film magazine has paid me to write a review. I scribble lots of notes as I watch, and I analyze everything, including the plot, the dialogue, the cast, the film score (background music), and the cinematography (camera angles, lighting, and effects).

4

The movie is action-packed, and I've got a lot to say about it. I loved the special effects, the costumes, and the story arc, but I found the cliffhanger ending frustrating. Tomorrow I'll turn my notes into a proper review. I'll have to summarize the story, without giving away any spoilers, and I'll also talk about the pros and cons. I think I'll give this one 4 stars!

MY JOB: BEST AND WORST PARTS

BEST: I get to see all the latest movies.

WORST: It's tough giving a bad review when I know so many people have worked so hard.

31

LOCATION SCOUT

I think my job is the best! I get to travel the world in search of incredible buildings and places for movies. The right location helps bring a fictional world to life and makes the story more believable. You don't need formal training for my job, but photography experience, a love of travel, and speaking multiple languages are all useful skills.

1

I'm currently working on finding locations for a movie called *Stranded in Space*. It's about a team of astronauts who crash on a desolate planet and learn to survive there. I've already read the script, spoken to the director about his vision, and started researching. Today, I'm visiting a potential location.

As a location scout, it's my job to find the perfect place to film movies, TV shows, commercials, and music videos. Once the locations have been approved, the location manager takes over, organizing everything from paying property owners, getting permits, and letting nearby residents know what's happening, to making sure the locations are returned to the same conditions after filming. For some projects, I work as both the scout and the manager.

2

During the drive from the hotel to the site, I make a few stops and take pictures of interesting buildings, neighborhoods, and roads. I'm always on the lookout for interesting locations that might work for a future scouting job.

3

Soon, I arrive at my destination: Death Valley National Park in California. It seems perfect! It's wild, empty, and goes on forever, without a building or road in sight. The desert sand dunes and mountains really give it an otherworldly atmosphere. I start taking photos and videos.

4

In addition to having the right look, a location needs to be practical. I speak to a park ranger who gives me useful information about the climate, terrain, and wildlife. I make notes about how much space there is for the crew and equipment, whether it's noisy, whether there's lots of natural light, whether we'll need generators to power the equipment, and whether there are hotels nearby for the cast and crew to stay in during the shoot.

5

Since it's a national park, we'll need a permit to film. I make a note of this, too. It's part of my job to find out if a location needs a permit, or permission from the owners, and to find out what the costs might be.

6

When I've finished, I head back to my hotel, but my work doesn't stop. There are more locations to find. Some scenes in the movie will be flashbacks of the astronauts on Earth, and I need to find a family home, a diner, and a sports stadium. I have a database of locations I've used in the past, so I check it first, and I also email a few contacts in real estate who might know of suitable locations.

7

I make a list of potential locations, then plot them on a map. For this movie, I've been asked to find sites that are close to each other to limit how much travel the cast and crew must do. For other jobs, I've had to find a regal palace in India, a lush tropical forest, and I once had to find a street in Los Angeles that had to look and feel like a street in Barcelona, Spain. Each brief is unique, and I love it!

8

After a few hours I decide to turn in for the night. Tomorrow I'm driving to another location. There's a scene in the movie where the astronauts are chased through caverns by angry aliens, and I've heard of some caverns in the Mojave Desert that could work as the location. Once I've found options for all the locations on my list, I'll share my notes and footage with the team, and revisit the sites with the director. If the locations are approved, my job is done; if they're not approved, it's back to the search!

MY JOB: BEST AND WORST PARTS

BEST: I feel lucky to visit so many interesting places.

WORST: It can be harder than you think trying to get permission to film in some locations.

POP SINGER

I spend my days doing my dream job: singing and recording songs, entertaining audiences, and working with other talented artists and professionals. But it took hard work to get here! I took singing lessons, put on performances, built my fan base on social media, and sent my work to record labels, before I finally got my big break. You need talent, patience, and a thick skin in my job.

I'm a solo artist, and my voice is my main instrument. Some singers prefer to be part of a group with other singers and musicians, and some work as backup singers for other artists. Not all singers sing pop music, like me—there are many genres, such as country, rock, and hip-hop.

1

This morning, I'm working on a new song. Sometimes I work with songwriters, but this one is one of my own, called "Best Friends." It's about my closest friend from my hometown. Singing songs that have a personal meaning helps audiences believe and connect with me. When the song is finished, I'll share it with my team at the record label, then record it.

2

My manager calls. His job is to help me succeed in my career, and he advises me on decisions, helps organize tours, and makes sure I'm treated fairly by my record label. He's excited because one of my songs, "Living the Good Life," is moving up the charts. He thinks I should make a music video to help the song gain even more attention. I happily agree!

4

At the venue, I do a sound check and rehearse. I'll be singing, dancing, and playing the guitar during the concert—having multiple talents helps me stand out.

3

Next, it's time to hit the road. I'm singing at a concert tonight, and it's a three-hour drive away. A lot of my time is spent traveling to venues and going on tour. I do a quick phone interview with a magazine and post on my social media accounts while the chauffeur drives—engaging with the media and my fans is super important.

star pop

5

Before I know it, it's showtime. I walk on stage and start to sing ...

MY JOB: BEST AND WORST PARTS

BEST: It's amazing to sing songs people might remember for the rest of their lives.

WORST: It's never nice to read that critics or the public don't like one of my songs.

MUSIC PRODUCER

I help artists create polished songs and albums. It's my job to know the music industry, current trends, and technology, and use that knowledge to help artists make hits. It's a varied job with lots of responsibility. I hire musicians, guide artists, make decisions about song arrangements, oversee the recording, and much more.

I earned a degree in music production, then worked as a production assistant, learning the skills and making contacts. Now, I'm a freelance music producer. Other producers work in-house for record labels and recording studios.

1

First up, I listen to a few demo tapes I've been sent by artists who want to work with me. These are samples of the artist's music that they have recorded themselves. If I don't know the genre of music well enough or can't connect with the sound, I know it's not the right fit. One of the tapes really stands out, so I call to arrange a meeting with the band and their manager.

2

Next, I'm recording a song with Joe Diamond, a solo artist. I booked the studio, musicians, and backup singers in advance, and we've already got the lyrics and melody decided. It's time to start playing! I listen to the song, and it doesn't feel right. We want a brash, bold sound, so I suggest we add some electric guitar and louder backup vocals to the chorus. The new arrangement is so much better.

3

We record the song multiple times, and I encourage Joe to try singing different notes and to really focus on his emotions as he sings. A big part of my role is to click with the artists and help them develop their sound. Later, I'll choose the best recordings and hire an engineer to mix it all together to create the best possible version.

4

My last task of the day is to meet with a rock band I just produced an album with. We're almost finished, but we can't agree on which order the songs should be in. They think the first song should be mellow and the last should be loud, but I think the opposite. In the end, they trust my judgement. Phew!

MY JOB: BEST AND WORST PARTS

BEST: I get to be involved in every part of creating music.

WORST: I feel a lot of pressure—artists trust me to get it right, and I never want to let them down.

CHOREOGRAPHER

My job is all about telling stories and expressing ideas through the art of dance. I work for a dance company, and I split my time between teaching the dancers routines and coming up with new ones. I trained as a dancer throughout my childhood and went on to earn a degree in dance. I learned about different dance styles, techniques, and theories, as well as the history of dance. Now, I get to create routines and watch others bring them to life.

Not all choreographers work for dance companies: many choreograph dance routines for music videos, concerts, commercials, TV shows, or movies.

1

Today, I'm working with the dancers. Our company specializes in jazz and contemporary dance styles, and we're working on a new production. I start by talking about the story, and the emotions we want the audience to feel as they watch. The production is about an adventure that two mice go on. It's whimsical, dramatic, and fun!

2

Next, I teach the steps for the first dance in the production (there are eight to learn in total). I play the music and we practice again and again. I give notes and tips as I watch. We'll continue rehearsing most days, right up until the first performance in three months.

3

In the afternoon, I work with the two lead dancers. They will be the mice, while the other dancers are cats. I explain how the dance steps should remind the audience of mice scampering around. In the coming weeks I'll ask the dancers to rehearse in costume, too, so I can see how the materials move with the steps. There's a lot to consider when choreographing, including costumes, props, lighting, and space.

4

It's almost the end of the day, so I ask all the dancers to practice once more while I film them. The artistic director stops by to watch, too. I often work closely with her, hiring dancers and planning productions.

5

I thank the dancers for their hard work and head home. It feels good to be off my feet! I watch the recording to see if anything needs changing. It's a great start, but it'll take time to perfect ... and, after that, there are seven more dances to learn!

MY JOB: BEST AND WORST PARTS

BEST: I love including new moves and techniques in my routines.

WORST: I don't like to see dancers get upset after I critique them. I always try to be constructive and fair.

BALLET DANCER

I started ballet classes when I was three, and I've been dancing ever since! I worked hard to get into a performing arts school where the teachers helped me develop my craft. Now I get to live my dream and dance in a professional company. My job takes a lot of hard work and determination. I get tired and I make mistakes ... but I just keep learning and dancing!

Ballet isn't the only option for people who love to dance. There are many styles and many opportunities. Some ballroom dancers travel the world competing for prizes, some hip-hop dancers go on tour with musicians, and jazz and tap dancers often work in musicals.

1

Tonight, I'll be on stage dancing in a production of *Sleeping Beauty*, but my day starts much earlier. I start work at 10:00 a.m., with ballet class. This is a chance to warm up my muscles before the day ahead—it's so important to take care of my body.

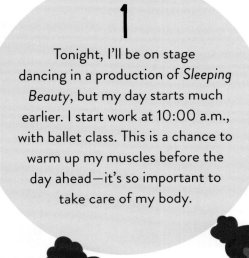

2

Next up, we're rehearsing for *The Nutcracker*, our next production after *Sleeping Beauty*. I'm in the "corps de ballet," which is the level most professional ballet dancers start at, and I mainly dance smaller parts and in group dances. One day, I hope to be a principal dancer—the highest level. The choreographers give me corrections and advice as I practice, and I rehearse for the next five hours! But my day's not over yet ...

3

After dinner, I go to the theater to get ready for tonight's performance. I get dressed and warm up again, and soon it's time to dance. The curtain rises, the music starts, and we begin.

4

The production lasts for two and a half hours, and I have multiple costume changes. It all goes by in a flash. At the end of the night, I leave the theater and overhear an audience member describing our moves as effortless—if only they knew!

MY JOB: BEST AND WORST PARTS

BEST: There are lots of people helping me to be the best dancer I can possibly be.

WORST: Sore muscles and banged-up feet are something dancers have to learn to live with.

VLOGGER

As a vlogger, I create videos about my life and interests and post them on social media. It's an amazing job—I get to choose when and where I work and talk about the things I love most. You don't need any formal training to start a vlog, just a camera and an idea, but to be successful isn't easy. You need talent, filming and editing skills, a strong work ethic, and lots of self-motivation.

Some people get confused between vloggers and bloggers. The letter "v" can help you to remember that vloggers make videos and bloggers write articles. Podcasters have similar jobs, but they create audio recordings that people can listen to.

1

Today, I'm in my friend's home filming her pet mice for my next vlog. Some vloggers post daily, but I post a vlog once a week. I love animals, and my vlogs are all about my pets and my friends' pets. I have a dog, a cat, a budgie, and an iguana. It's so important to pick the right topic to vlog about. Your viewers will only be enthusiastic if you are.

2

I start by filming the mice as they scurry around. They're really cute, so this will be a fun video to watch. I use a good quality camera and a tripod to keep it steady to record the footage because nobody wants to watch shaky, unfocused videos! If I'm not planning to film, but I spot an opportunity, I'll often use my smartphone camera, which is also good quality, and easier to carry around.

HOW DO VLOGGERS MAKE MONEY?

Vloggers make money from their videos in three main ways:

1. Advertising—this is where ads are inserted at various points of the video. The more people who watch or click on the ad, the more money the vlogger receives.

2. Sponsorships—successful vloggers with lots of subscribers can be paid by companies to mention their products in videos.

3. Affiliate marketing—this is where vloggers include links or coupons for other companies in their videos. If viewers buy the products, the vlogger gets paid.

In all cases, the more subscribers a vlogger has, the easier it will be for them to earn money.

3

Next, I record myself interviewing my friend about her choice of pet. I have my questions prepared in advance. This helps my vlogs feel professional, and means I don't get stuck searching for the right thing to say. There are millions of videos online, so mine need to be as good as they possibly can. Once I've finished recording, I thank my friend before I head home.

4

I record audio clips of myself talking about mice, giving facts and information—I also have a few mouse jokes ready to slip in. My favorite is "Why don't elephants use computers? Because they're afraid of the mouse!" Getting your personality across is so important in vlogging, and helps viewers connect with you. I'm known for my silly jokes, so I always make sure to include one or two.

5

But my work's not over! Now, it's time for the editing. I use special software to arrange my recordings in the order I want, add in the audio clips, and add music and text. Good editing can really make a vlog shine, but it takes time, care, and patience to get everything perfect.

6

Finally, it's time to click "upload" and share my vlog with the world. I post about the vlog on all my social media accounts, too, to let friends, family, and followers know it's up. I have to work hard to make sure my vlogs get seen. This is why I start every vlog by asking viewers to subscribe to and click "like" on my vlogs.

7

I finish the day looking through the comments from my viewers. I recently asked them to comment on what my next vlog should be about. Communicating with viewers like this helps them stay interested and feel like they're part of the vlog. I can see that many of them have asked for a vlog about Arnold, my iguana—he's got lots of fans!

MY JOB: BEST AND WORST PARTS

BEST: I love talking to viewers and fans from all over the world.

WORST: Sometimes people leave unkind comments, which can be hard to see. I always remind myself that their words don't matter, and turn to my family and friends for support when I need it.

MOVIE DIRECTOR

As a movie director, it's my job to turn a script into a movie. This involves everything from managing how the scenes are filmed, and overseeing the music, costumes, and locations, to approving the final, edited movie. I studied filmmaking in college, and made my own short films. Then I worked as an assistant director on small productions and bigger movies. Now, I'm directing a big-budget, feature-length movie set in the American West of the 19th Century.

When the movie credits roll, you will often see the name of the director and the producer. The director manages the creative side, while the producer looks after the business side. This can include finding the right script, making sure the movie stays on budget, and promoting the movie to the media and the public.

1

A director's work begins long before filming starts. I worked with the art department to research the period and setting of the film, and today the first thing I do is check the set and props to make sure everything looks right.

2

Next, I look at the schedule. I have to be organized and ensure that the right people are in the right place at the right time. Today, we need the lead actor, his character's family, extras to play the villagers, and the film crew, including camera operators and sound technicians.

3

The casting director has picked great actors, and the whole cast has come prepared. There's time for a few rehearsals before we start filming, so we run through the scene. I give the actors direction, encouraging them to try the scene in different ways until we find the perfect one. This can take a while, and some of the actors get frustrated. I reassure them that the movie will be better because we've tried out different ideas. My job is all about leadership and motivating people.

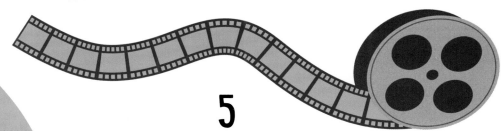

4

Next, I speak with the camera operators to explain that the end of the scene should move from a close-up of the boy and his mother to a shot showing the wide, open plain. We follow a storyboard drawn up by the storyboard artist (under my direction), where every shot of the movie is sketched out. I've worked hard on my communication skills so that I can share my thoughts.

5

Finally, I think we're ready to shoot the scene. I sit behind the camera and watch as it plays out, making sure the acting, lighting, props, and set are all perfect. If I want the scene to end, I yell "Cut!" We often do multiple takes, filming the same scene several times to get it right.

6

I'm pleased with the first take, but I ask for another. I want the mother character to look a little more tearful as her son walks off into the distance. The actor disagrees: she thinks her character would be sad, but also proud of her son and wouldn't cry. I listen to her ideas, but decide to stick with my gut. Making decisions like this is part of my job.

MY JOB: BEST AND WORST PARTS

BEST: I'm there every step of the way on a movie's journey from script to screen, and it's great to see everyone's hard work pay off.

WORST: Often unexpected challenges come up—like faulty equipment or actors having a bad day—and it's up to me to solve the problems.

7

The second take is much better. I watch the film, and I'm really excited! It will look fantastic after I work on it with the editor in the studio. I make sure to praise the actors, and tell them how pleased I am. "That's a wrap!" I shout. A huge cheer goes up. It took ten exhausting hours for two minutes of film. That sounds like a lot, but I never, ever settle for anything less than perfect.

RADIO DJ

Growing up, I often went on road trips with my dad, and we'd spend the time listening to the radio. That's where my love of music began! Later, I earned a degree in broadcast journalism. My studies helped me develop skills, including how to use recording equipment and how to conduct interviews. I worked for my college radio station, then interned at a local radio station and worked my way up. Today, I'm a DJ for CoolTunes FM, a popular radio station.

You need good speaking skills, confidence, and lots of personality in my job, since it's all about talking and connecting with listeners.

1

I arrive at the station at 5:00 a.m. I work the morning shift, and early starts are normal for me! My show begins at 7:00 a.m., so I use the extra time to check in with the program director (she's in charge of all the station's shows, including mine). Together, we run through the plan for today—it's a special show since I'll be interviewing a new singer.

2

Next, I chat to the music director (his job is to choose the songs I'll be playing, which is called the playlist). I look at today's playlist and make notes on things I want to say between songs. I also check the news and social media, looking for anything I could talk about during the show. I often discuss new trends, current events ... and music, of course! Today, I read that a popular band is breaking up, so we quickly add one of the band's songs to the playlist.

4

It's time for my guest interview. I welcome the singer, and we talk about his album, his life, and the musicians that inspire him. I play one of his songs for the listeners. Interviews like this are typical in my job, so I can't get starstruck; I have to keep my cool!

3

Finally, I'm on the air. The time flies as I play the songs and talk. I also take song requests from callers and announce a new competition we are running over the next two weeks: listeners can call in and guess the name of the song we're playing—but they only get to listen for 3 seconds! The winner gets the chance to come in and host the show with me.

5

At 10:30 a.m., my show comes to an end. I'll be back tomorrow morning, but this afternoon, I'm going to a music festival on behalf of the station. Keeping up-to-date with the latest music is a big part of my job, so I often attend events like this.

TICKET

MY JOB: BEST AND WORST PARTS

BEST: I get to talk about my favorite thing—music!

WORST: My show is live, so I can't afford to make mistakes. It can be stressful.

SESSION MUSICIAN

I started to play the flute when I was in elementary school, and I picked up the saxophone in high school. I loved both instruments and wanted to make a career out of my talent, so I became a session musician. I spend my days playing and recording music for bands, solo artists, TV commercials, and movie scores, as well as performing live.

1

This morning, I'm working with a pop band called Dreamclouds. They are recording a new album that needs a saxophone player on a few tracks, and that's where I come in! I've been hired to play and record with them. I've worked for the band's record label before, and made a good impression, which is why they've hired me again today. As a freelancer, I work for myself, so building a good reputation is key.

2

The session goes well. I read the music and play my parts with passion. The band aren't sure about one of the songs, and they ask me if I have any ideas. I improvise and change some of the notes, and they love it.

You don't need formal training for my job, but it can be helpful. I studied from a young age and earned a degree in music. This helped me to develop my skills in sight-reading and playing different genres, and taught me about music theory and history.

3

Back at home, I check my email, do paperwork, and schedule more jobs. While I'm at my desk, I receive a call from Dreamclouds' record label. The band were so impressed that they want me to join them on tour next summer, playing live on the songs we recorded earlier today. I jump at the chance. Tours are always great fun!

4

Next, I turn my attention to tomorrow's job. I've been hired to play the flute for a song that will feature in a TV commercial. Playing more than one instrument gives me more opportunities for work. I've been sent the music for tomorrow's song already, so I pick up my flute and spend the next three hours practicing. You can never practice enough in my job!

MY JOB: BEST AND WORST PARTS

BEST: I get to work with lots of different singers, musicians, and musical styles.

WORST: Even if a song I've worked on is a big hit, most people never know I helped to make it!

uly

On tour!

43

YOUR PERFECT JOB MATCH

With so many jobs out there, it can be tricky to choose between them. Use this guide to find out which careers match up with your skills, personal qualities, and interests.

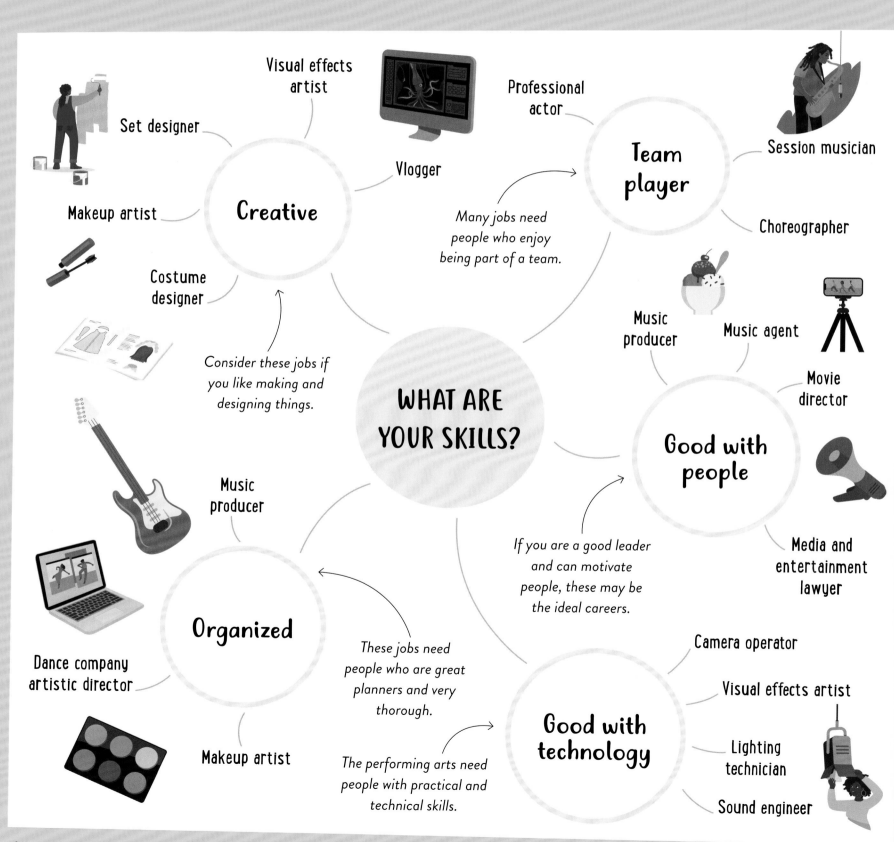

Visual effects artist

Set designer

Vlogger

Professional actor

Creative

Team player

Session musician

Choreographer

Makeup artist

Costume designer

Consider these jobs if you like making and designing things.

Many jobs need people who enjoy being part of a team.

Music producer

Music agent

Movie director

WHAT ARE YOUR SKILLS?

Good with people

Music producer

If you are a good leader and can motivate people, these may be the ideal careers.

Media and entertainment lawyer

Organized

Dance company artistic director

These jobs need people who are great planners and very thorough.

Camera operator

Visual effects artist

Good with technology

Lighting technician

Makeup artist

The performing arts need people with practical and technical skills.

Sound engineer

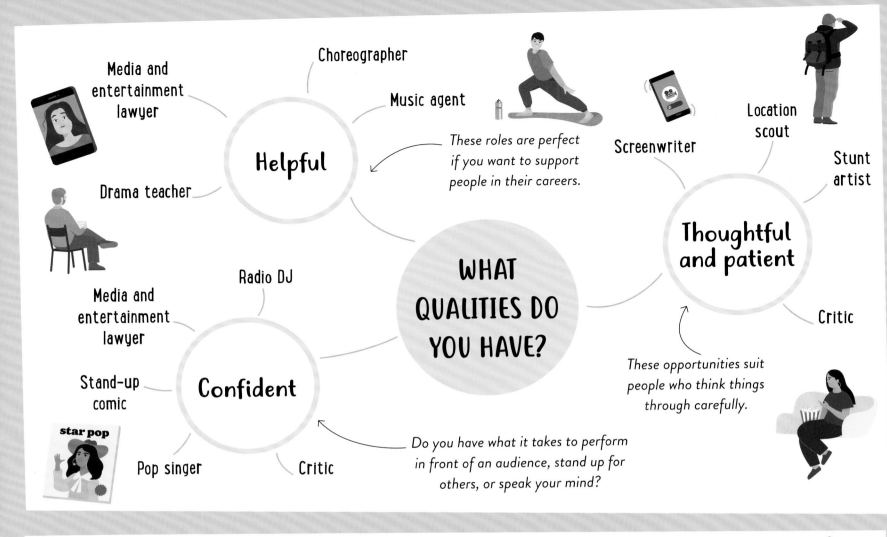

Helpful
- Media and entertainment lawyer
- Choreographer
- Music agent
- Drama teacher

These roles are perfect if you want to support people in their careers.

Confident
- Radio DJ
- Media and entertainment lawyer
- Stand-up comic
- Pop singer
- Critic

Do you have what it takes to perform in front of an audience, stand up for others, or speak your mind?

WHAT QUALITIES DO YOU HAVE?

Thoughtful and patient
- Screenwriter
- Location scout
- Stunt artist
- Critic

These opportunities suit people who think things through carefully.

star pop

Fame
- Professional actor
- Pop singer
- Stand-up comic
- Radio DJ

If you love the limelight, these are the choices for you.

WHAT ARE YOUR INTERESTS AND GOALS?

Some performing arts jobs need people to be fit and healthy.

Keeping active
- Ballet dancer
- Camera operator
- Stunt artist

Bringing ideas to life
- Screenwriter
- Vlogger
- Movie director
- Set designer
- Session musician

If you like seeing what's in your head appear in the real world, perhaps your future lies here.

Travel
- Location scout
- Professional actor
- Stunt artist

You could visit many exciting locations in these jobs.

45

THERE'S MORE...

You've already read about a huge number of exciting opportunities in the world of performing arts, but there are even more to choose from! You can read about some of them here.

SHOWRUNNER

A successful TV show might run for years, have hundreds of episodes, and employ a vast number of writers, actors, and other professionals. A showrunner's job is to make sure each episode is made on time, and on budget, and that the cast are happy, and the crew is working well. It's a job for someone who loves being a leader.

CIRCUS PERFORMER

A circus performer entertains audiences with incredible acts. There are different types of circus performers, including acrobats, tightrope walkers, trapeze artists, and aerial artists. Most circus performers spend lots of time developing and practicing routines. They can perform in different settings, including festivals, in theaters, and on cruise ships, either as solo artists or as part of a group. If you like travel, keeping fit, and excitement, this could be the job for you!

SONGWRITER

Professional songwriters write songs for singers and bands to perform. Many famous artists use songwriters, and often work with the same ones again and again. Some songwriters write the music and lyrics, while others only write one or the other. Songwriters might work for themselves, selling songs to performers, or they might work in-house for a music publisher. Writing skills are key for this job.

EVENT MANAGER

Have you ever enjoyed a music festival in your local park or been to a big arts event? These don't just happen by themselves. Somebody has to book performers, schedule venues, let the media know what's happening, set up ticket sales, manage staff, make sure everything is ready on the day, and manage the cleanup at the end. It's definitely a job for someone who is good at organizing!

FILM EDITOR

Movies and TV shows are filmed in small sections, called "scenes." It's the film editor's job to watch all the footage, work with the director to decide which parts to keep and which to cut, and then use video-editing software to put everything together to create a complete movie or episode. It's the perfect job for someone who wants to use their creative flair and their technical skills.

FILM SCORE COMPOSER

Music is very important in a movie. It can set the mood and change how the audience feels. Film score composers work closely with a movie's director to decide which scenes need music, and what moods the director wants to create. They then write the music and record it using hired performers or musical software. Often the music is written to complement the story, so a big moment might be accompanied by lots of dramatic music. If you love music and can work as part of a team, you might be suited to this job.

SPOKEN WORD ARTIST

If you love everything about words, a career as a spoken word artist could be perfect. These performers read their poetry in front of audiences and might even include music to help create the perfect atmosphere. You need to be creative as well as confident speaking in front of crowds to succeed in this job.

First American Edition 2022
Kane Miller, A Division of EDC Publishing

For information contact:
Kane Miller, A Division of EDC Publishing
5402 S 122nd E Ave, Tulsa, OK 74146
www.kanemiller.com
www.myubam.com

Library of Congress Control Number: 2021944885

Manufactured in Guangdong, China CC0322

ISBN: 978-1-68464-287-8

1 2 3 4 5 6 7 8 9 10